Donated by Alice Elgart
In honor of the Steering Committee of
*The Campaign for Allen-Stevenson:
Today and Tomorrow*

LARRY DIERKER
CRAIG BIGGIO
JOSE CRUZ
JIM WYNN
SHANE REYNOLDS
BOB WATSON
JEFF BAGWELL
NOLAN RYAN
BILLY WAGNER
CESAR CEDENO
J.R. RICHARD
LANCE BERKMAN

THE HISTORY OF THE

HOUSTON
ASTROS

MICHAEL E. GOODMAN

CREATIVE C EDUCATION

Published by Creative Education, 123 South Broad Street, Mankato, MN 56001

Creative Education is an imprint of The Creative Company.

Designed by Rita Marshall.

Photographs by AllSport (Brian Bahr, David Seelig), Associated Press/Wide World Photos, FotoSport

(Mitch Reibel), SportsChrome (Rob Tringali Jr.)

Library of Congress Cataloging-in-Publication Data

Goodman, Michael E. The history of the Houston Astros / by Michael Goodman.

p. cm. — (Baseball)   ISBN 1-58341-210-7

Summary: Highlights the key personalities and memorable games in the history of the

team that changed its name to the Astros in 1965 when it moved to the first indoor

baseball stadium, the Astrodome.

1. Houston Astros (Baseball team)—History—

Juvenile literature. [1. Houston Astros (Baseball team)—History.

2. Baseball—History.] 1. Title. II. Baseball (Mankato, Minn.).

GV875.H64 G655 2002   796.757'64'097641411—dc21   2001047883

First Edition 9 8 7 6 5 4 3 2 1

HOUSTON,

TEXAS, IS A CITY WITH A SPLIT PERSONALITY. PART OF

Houston's charactor is linked to its Old West past, and part is

connected to the space age by the presence of the Johnson Space

Center, headquarters of the National Aeronautics and Space

Administration (NASA). The city has long been a home for

cowboys and oilmen as well as physicists and astronauts.

The history of Houston's major league baseball team also

reflects both the past and present sides of the city. When the team

first joined the National League (NL) in 1962, it was called the Colt

.45s, after the most famous weapon of the Old West. Three years

later, the club's owners decided to update its image, choosing the

name Astros since Houston was the home of America's space

KEN JOHNSON

program. Since that time, the Astros have created a Texas-sized reputation for baseball excitement in the Southwest.

Outfielder Roman Mejias supplied most of the first-year Colt .45s' offense, driving in 76 runs.

{HEAT, MOSQUITOES, AND THE DOME}

The Colt .45s found little success early on. The club finished in eighth or ninth place in the 10-team National League in 1962, 1963, and 1964. Yet the team did provide its share of thrilling moments, such as the no-hitters recorded by pitchers Don Nottebart and Ken Johnson in 1963 and 1964.

During those early years, Houston fans did a lot of cheering and clapping. Partly, they were applauding the team's play. And, partly, they were trying to chase away the hordes of giant mosquitoes that buzzed around Colt Stadium on hot, humid Texas evenings. Players and fans could hardly wait for the team to move into its new domed stadium.

MOISES ALOU

A Houston star in the **1960s** and '**70s**, Larry Dierker returned as manager in the '**90s**.

LARRY DIERKER

That move, accompanied by some other key changes, occurred in April 1965. The Colt .45s became the Astros, players donned new uniforms with a streaking star across the chest, and the club changed its address to the remarkable Astrodome. The new stadium had a domed ceiling that rose 208 feet above the field (higher than an 18-story building), an internal weather station that kept the temperature a comfortable 72 degrees, and futuristic synthetic grass called Astro-Turf.

However, the team's new name, uniforms, and stadium didn't result in a big change in its success on the field. The club's pitching remained strong, especially the work of right-handers Don Wilson, who tossed two no-hitters, and Larry Dierker, the team's first 20-game winner. But the Astros' batters couldn't seem to get enough hits to win ball games.

Lefty Mike Cueller was superb on the mound in **1966**, ending the season with a 2.22 ERA.

9

MIKE CUELLER

Minute Maid Park, opened in 2000, was built to include a train and an 800-foot track.

MINUTE MAID PARK

Then, in the late 1960s, several fine hitters joined the squad, including slugging outfielder Jim Wynn. Wynn, whose nickname was the "Toy Cannon," amazed fans with the explosive power that his compact 5-foot-9 frame generated. When he was asked how he could hit the ball so far in the weather-controlled Astrodome, Wynn replied with a laugh, "Whenever I come to bat, the wind blows out...." Wynn's "wind-aided" power helped the Astros rise in the NL standings.

Infielders Roger Metzger and Joe Morgan were the NL's top triples hitters in **1971** (11 apiece).

12

{THE CESAR CEDENO STORY} Even with their improved hitting and strong pitching, the Astros never had a winning season in the 1960s. Then, after the 1971 season, the team's owners made some key trades, bringing in smooth-fielding second baseman Tommy Helms and power-hitting first baseman Lee May. The newcomers were one reason Houston recorded its first winning

CESAR CEDENO

season (84–69) in 1972.

The other key factor that season was the inspired play of a

22-year-old phenom from the Dominican Republic named Cesar

Cedeno. "There must be something Cedeno can't do well, but I

haven't found it yet," said Cincinnati Reds manager Sparky

Anderson. "Cedeno's speed gives me heartburn," added Cincinnati's

All-Star catcher Johnny Bench.

Cedeno could do it all. In 1972, he batted .320, hit 22 homers,

scored 103 runs, and racked up 82 RBI. He also stole

55 bases and won the first of five straight Gold Glove

awards for his defensive play in center field. The next

year, he became the first player in major-league history

to steal 50 bases and hit 20 homers in consecutive

14 seasons. Led by Cedeno, Wynn, Helms, first baseman Bob Watson,

and third baseman Doug Rader, the Astros became a force to be

reckoned with in the NL Western Division.

But a strange, troubling incident occurred just before the 1974

season. Cedeno was arrested in the Dominican Republic and

charged with killing his girlfriend there. He was released when it

was determined that his girlfriend had shot herself accidentally with

his gun. Cedeno rejoined the Astros, but the death seemed to haunt

MIKE HAMPTON

him. He continued to play solid baseball for many more years but never achieved true superstar status.

{J.R. AND THE LATE '70s} Another Houston player whose

career was tinged by tragedy was James Rodney (J.R.) Richard, the Astros' best pitcher in the late 1970s. At 6-foot-8 and 230 pounds, J.R. was truly a big star. He joined the club in 1975 and a year later became only its second 20-game winner. In 1978, he set a league

record as the first NL right-hander to strike out more than

300 batters in a season. Then, in 1979, Richard and

knuckleballer Joe Niekro helped lead the Astros to an

89–73 record—the best in club history—and a close

second-place finish behind Cincinnati.

In **1979**, J.R. Richard pitched 86 consecutive innings without the need for a relief pitcher.

Things were really looking up for Houston

when the team acquired American League strikeout king Nolan

Ryan, a Texas native, before the 1980 season. Both Ryan and

Richard got off to good starts in 1980, and Niekro was having his

best season ever. Then, on July 30, tragedy struck. During warm-

ups, Richard staggered and collapsed. He had suffered a stroke that

cut off oxygen to the right side of his brain. It took 18 hours of

delicate brain surgery to save Richard's life.

Later, resting in his hospital room, J.R. promised that he would

J.R. RICHARD

Like Cesar Cedeno, Craig Biggio was an Astros All-Star known for his sure glove.

come back soon. "It's just a matter of time," Richard predicted. "I see the progress. Meanwhile, I know Nolan Ryan and the rest of the team will never give up on this season." Richard was right about his teammates. Inspired by his courage, the Astros won 93 games and captured their first NL West title. Ryan struck out 200 batters, Niekro won 20 games, and Cedeno and fellow outfielder Jose Cruz led a hard-hitting lineup.

With a team-leading 91 RBI, outfielder Jose Cruz helped fuel Houston's great run in **1980**.

In the best-of-five NL Championship Series against Philadelphia, the Astros won twice but lost the deciding game in extra innings to fall just short of their first World Series berth. Sadly, Richard's battle did not have a happy ending either. He tried to make a comeback the next season but didn't have the same reflexes or speed on his fastball. He pitched some in the minor leagues and then retired from baseball.

20

JOSE CRUZ

{CRUZ-ING TOWARD A PENNANT} In 1981, Houston got

off to a slow start. However, a midseason strike led baseball officials

to split the season. The leader of each division in the first half of the

season would play the leader during the second half in a division

playoff. Given new life, the Astros went 32–20 during the second

half to earn a playoff spot against the Los Angeles Dodgers. As had happened the year before, the Astros took their opponent to a

deciding game five but came up short again.

From **1985** to **1989**, in-fielder Glenn Davis was Houston's top home run hitter every season.

Over the next five years, Houston stayed near the

top of the NL West. Astros fans saw some spectacular

pitching from Nolan Ryan, who set major-league

records by notching his fifth career no-hitter in 1981,

becoming baseball's all-time strikeout king in 1983,

and surpassing 4,000 career strikeouts during the 1985 season.

The team also featured several outstanding infielders during

those days, including Art Howe, Ray Knight, and Dickie Thon.

However, Houston fans reserved their loudest applause for left

fielder Jose Cruz.

Over a 13-year career in Houston (1975 to 1987), Cruz was the

team's most consistent offensive performer. He batted over .300

six times (three times after the age of 35) and was twice named to

GLENN DAVIS

One of base-
ball's legends,
Nolan Ryan
led the NL
in strikeouts
in **1987**
and **1988**.

NOLAN RYAN

the NL All-Star team. Cruz was a notorious bad-ball hitter.

"Throw the ball three feet over his head and outside, and he'll hit

it down the left-field line," said Dodgers pitcher Pat

Zachary. "Three feet over his head and inside, and he'll

go to right."

Led by Cruz and pitchers Mike Scott and Jim

Deshaies, the Astros made another push for the NL

pennant in 1986. Scott was particularly impressive all season,

topping off the year by hurling a no-hitter against the San Francisco

Giants to clinch the division title. For his work, the right-hander

won the NL Cy Young Award as the league's best pitcher.

The Astros then took on the New York Mets in the playoffs

in a classic battle. The Mets went up 3–2 in the best-of-seven series,

setting the stage for game six—one of the most exciting games

in playoff history. Houston jumped ahead 3–0, but New York

A great all-around player, Dickie Thon spent seven seasons with the Astros in the **1980s**.

25

DICKIE THON

outfielder Darryl Strawberry homered in the ninth to tie the game.

The contest went to the 16th inning, when the Mets scored three

times and barely held off a Houston rally to win the game and

the series 7–6.

{THE "KILLER B'S"} In the 1990s, the most important letter

in the alphabet for Houston fans was "B," as players named Biggio,

Bagwell, Bell, and Berry—collectively known as the "Killer B's"—

emerged as team leaders and helped the Astros rise to the top of the

NL Central Division.

Craig Biggio was the first to arrive. He joined

Houston in 1988 as a catcher but was soon switched

to second base because of his great speed. He adapted

quickly to the new position and won four consecutive

Gold Glove awards as the NL's best fielding second-sacker from

1994 to 1997. Biggio also made a name for himself at the plate,

becoming the team's career leader in hits, runs scored, and doubles.

Jeff Bagwell, another Killer B and the club's first baseman

starting in 1992, set nearly every Houston offensive record not

established by Biggio. The NL's Most Valuable Player (MVP) in

1994 and one of the league's most consistent stars throughout the

1990s, Bagwell became Houston's career leader in batting average,

In **1994**, Jeff Bagwell won the Gold Glove award for his defense and blasted 39 home runs.

JEFF BAGWELL

home runs, extra-base hits, and RBI.

Between 1996 and 2001, Bagwell cemented his superstar status by recording six consecutive 30-plus home run, 100-plus RBI seasons. He also developed into a top fielder and base runner. According to Oakland Athletics manager Art Howe, "Jeff Bagwell has the best baseball instincts of anybody I've seen since [Giants Hall of Fame outfielder] Willie Mays."

In **1996**, Derek Bell and Jeff Bagwell made club history, each driving in more than 100 runs.

Biggio and Bagwell were joined in Houston in the mid-1990s by the other Killer Bs— outfielder Derek Bell and third baseman Sean Berry—to form an exciting offensive nucleus. In the next few years, Houston also added such players as starting pitchers Shane Reynolds, Mike Hampton, and Jose Lima; closer Billy Wagner; outfielders Richard Hidalgo and Moises Alou; and catcher Brad Ausmus. These players helped Houston win consecutive NL Central

DEREK BELL

titles in 1997, 1998, and 1999.

{A NEW HOME IN A NEW CENTURY} The year 2000 marked more than just the start of a new century for the Astros. It was also the year in which the club moved to its new home, Enron Field (named Minute Maid Park in 2002). A club-record three million fans came out in 2000 to watch the Astros in their new stadium. And although the squad suffered its first losing season since 1991, there were a number of highlights. Bagwell set new club records with 47 home runs and 152 runs scored, the team established new single-season highs for home runs and RBI, and Reynolds was selected to pitch in his first All-Star Game.

The Astros also added a new Killer B: left fielder Lance Berkman. An All-American out of Rice University in Houston, Berkman was a switch-hitter with exceptional power from both

In one of Houston's best-ever pitching performances, Billy Wagner recorded 39 saves in **1999**.

29

BILLY WAGNER

Power-hitting outfielder Lance Berkman was one of the NL's fastest-rising stars.

LANCE BERKMAN

Burly right fielder Richard Hidalgo averaged 101 RBI a season in **2000** and **2001**.

RICHARD HIDALGO

sides of the plate. When he joined Hidalgo and Alou in the Houston outfield, the Astros suddenly had the NL's top offensive outfield

trio. All three players turned it on in 2001, helping the Astros to win their division and reach the playoffs once more.

Major league baseball in Houston has come a long way since the days of the Colt .45s with their weak

bats and giant mosquitoes. First, the gunslingers were transformed into space-age Astros and soared to the top of the National League. Now, in their new home and with a new winning attitude, the 21st-century Astros are hoping to reach new heights of excellence.

WADE MILLER

Math in the Real World

How Chefs Use Math

By Sheri L. Arroyo

Math Curriculum Consultant: Rhea A. Stewart, M.A.,
Specialist in Mathematics, Science,
and Technology Education

CHELSEA CLUBHOUSE

An Imprint of Chelsea House Publishers

Chelsea Clubhouse
An imprint of Chelsea House Publishers
132 West 31st Street
New York NY 10001

Library of Congress Cataloging-in-Publication Data
Arroyo, Sheri L.
        How chefs use math / by Sheri L. Arroyo; math curriculum consultant, Rhea A. Stewart.
            p. cm. — (Math in the real world)
        Includes bibliographical references and index.
        ISBN 978-1-60413-608-1
        1. Mathematics—Study and teaching (Elementary—Activity programs—Juvenile literature.
        2. Cookery—Juvenile literature. I. Title. II. Series.
    QA135.6.A77 2010
    513.076—dc22   2009014180

Chelsea Clubhouse books are available at special discounts when purchased in bulk quantities for businesses, associations, institutions, or sales promotions. Please call our Special Sales Department in New York at (212) 967-8800 or (800) 322-8755.

You can find Chelsea Clubhouse on the World Wide Web at http://www.chelseahouse.com

Developed for Chelsea House by RJF Publishing LLC (www.RJFpublishing.com)
Text and cover design by Tammy West/Westgraphix LLC
Illustrations by Spectrum Creative Inc.
Photo research by Edward A. Thomas
Index by Nila Glikin

Photo Credits: 4: Jon Feingersh/Photolibrary; 6: © Roy McMahon/Corbis; 8, 10, 24: AP/Wide World Photos; 12: Index Stock Imagery/Photolibrary; 14: David Woolley/Taxi (Getty Images); 16: Jonathan Perugia/Time Out/Photolibrary; 18: Steve Mason/Photolibrary; 20: Reuters/Landov; 22: © Tim Pannell/Corbis; 26: Getty Images.

Printed and bound in the United States of America

Bang RJF 10 9 8 7 6 5 4 3 2 1

This book is printed on acid-free paper.

All links and Web addresses were checked and verified to be correct at the time of publication. Because of the dynamic nature of the Web, some addresses and links may have changed since publication and may no longer be valid.

Table of Contents

Answers and helpful hints for the You Do the Math
activities are in the Answer Key.

Words that are defined in the Glossary are
in **bold** type the first time they appear in the text.

The Business of Cooking

Do you like to cook? Do you like to try new foods or help create special dishes for your friends and family? Are you good at **estimating**, adding, and measuring? Then you might like to become a chef!

Kinds of Chefs

There are many different kinds of chefs. Most chefs work in restaurants. Many people start out as a "line cook" in a restaurant, making soups, salads, fish, or meat. After a while, a good chef may become the restaurant's executive chef. The executive chef plans the menu and

A chef takes freshly baked bread out of the oven at a restaurant.

buys the food. She watches over the kitchen to be sure everything runs smoothly. Some chefs even open their own restaurants.

Some people work as personal chefs. A personal chef may cook for individuals or families at their homes. A personal chef may also work at a company's office. Caterers are chefs who make food for special occasions, such as weddings.

All of these people love to cook. They are also good at math. They have to be—they need to use math every day.

You Do the Math

Cooking Time

It's important for a chef to plan carefully, so that all the dishes that have to be served at the same time finish cooking at the same time. The table below shows dishes a chef is making for a dinner. If dinner will be served at 6:30 P.M., what time does each dish need to be put in the oven so that it will be done cooking at 6:30?

What's for Dinner	
Dish	**Cooking Time (in minutes)**
Cheese potatoes	75
Glazed carrots	30
Bread pudding	60
Roast chicken	120
Buttermilk biscuits	20
Pumpkin bread	50

Now, put the dishes in **sequential order**, beginning with the first dish that needs to go into the oven.

Kitchen Math

A chef has to do a lot more than cook delicious things to eat. An important part of her job is making sure that she cooks just the right amount of food. She doesn't want to throw away extra food. After all, **ingredients** cost money, and no one wants to waste food. To avoid waste, a chef often needs to **convert**, or change, **recipe** ingredient amounts, so that enough—but not too much—food is cooked.

Converting Recipes

A chef cooking a special dinner decides to make chocolate cookies for dessert. Her recipe makes enough for ten people. If only five guests are coming for dinner, she will need to reduce the amounts of all the ingredients by half. If twenty guests are coming, she will need to double the amounts of all of the ingredients in the recipe so that there will be enough. The table on the next page shows how much is one-half and how much is double (two times as much) for common measurements.

This chef is carefully measuring the amount of flour that will go into a recipe.

One-Half and Double Measurements		
Measurement	$\frac{1}{2}$ Measurement	Double Measurement
1 cup	$\frac{1}{2}$ cup	2 cups
$\frac{1}{4}$ cup	$\frac{1}{8}$ cup	$\frac{1}{2}$ cup
$\frac{1}{2}$ cup	$\frac{1}{4}$ cup	1 cup
$1\frac{1}{2}$ cups	$\frac{3}{4}$ cup	3 cups

The chef needs to be careful to increase or decrease the amounts of all ingredients in proportion to each other. If she doubles one ingredient, she has to double every ingredient so the recipe turns out the way it should.

You Do the Math

Converting a Recipe

Now you try it! Use the table above to help you convert the amounts of the ingredients for these recipes.

How much do you need of each ingredient if you are doubling this recipe for oatmeal raisin cookies?

1 egg

1 cup brown sugar

$1\frac{1}{2}$ cups oats

$\frac{1}{2}$ cup butter

2 tablespoons milk

$\frac{1}{4}$ cup raisins

How much do you need of each ingredient to make half of this recipe for French toast?

4 slices bread

2 eggs

$\frac{1}{2}$ cup milk

2 tablespoons butter

Cooking Supplies

When a chef walks into the kitchen each day, he'll first check his food supplies. He will see how much he has of different ingredients. He will also make sure that all the food is fresh and safe to use. Then he will **calculate** how much of the different ingredients he needs for the recipes he's cooking today.

Dry ingredients—such as flour, sugar, beans, rice, and spices—stay fresh longer than other ingredients. The chef will not need to buy these items very often. He can buy a lot at one time and keep them on hand. Fresh ingredients—such as eggs, milk, fish, meat, fruits, and vegetables—can spoil, or become unusable, quickly. The chef must buy these in smaller amounts every day or two.

In the walk-in refrigerator in his restaurant, a chef checks his fruits and vegetables to make sure they are still fresh.

Watching the Temperature

A chef must be sure that all of his food is kept cold enough so that it stays fresh and safe to eat for as long as possible. He does not want to have to throw away food that has spoiled. He checks the **thermometers** every day in the places where he keeps food. Fresh vegetables, milk, and meat need to be kept **refrigerated** at a temperature no higher than 41 degrees Fahrenheit (F). Dry foods can be stored in the pantry at a temperature up to 70 degrees F. Seafood needs to be kept refrigerated at a temperature no higher than 34 degrees F.

You Do the Math

Cold Enough?

Think about the best temperature for storing each of the foods listed in the table below. The current temperature for each food is given in the table. How many degrees must the chef lower the temperature for each of the first three foods in order for each item to be stored safely? How many degrees can the temperature of each of the last two items go up for these items to still be stored safely in the pantry?

Food and Temperature	
Food	**Temperature (in degrees F)**
Roast Beef	48
Shrimp	60
Lettuce	51
Flour	45
Sugar	60

Buying the Food

How does a chef get the ingredients to make the dishes that are on the menu? Sometimes, he will work with a food **purveyor**. A food purveyor is someone who brings food to the restaurant. For example, a fish purveyor will bring fresh seafood to the chef. Before the chef orders food, he will ask how much each item costs. The chef has a budget, which is how much money he can spend. So, he needs to make careful decisions about the foods he buys.

At a fresh food market, this chef is checking out what looks especially good.

Fresh Food Markets

A chef might also shop for certain ingredients on her own. For example, she might get up early in the morning to visit the fresh food market. After seeing what ingredients look especially good, she might decide what she's going to cook as she's shopping! She will ask how much things cost, too. She might have to pick something different if an item she wants costs more than her budget will allow.

Help the Chef Shop

A chef needs to buy chicken or fish, vegetables, and fruit for dessert. The list below shows different foods and how much each item costs.

Food Items and Costs	
Item	**Cost**
4 chickens	$17.00
8 fresh trout	$24.00
2 bags red potatoes	$12.00
6 avocados	$17.00
10 bunches carrots	$20.00
6 baskets strawberries	$24.00
6 baskets cherries	$35.00

You have $70.00 to spend. Which of the following three groups of items can you buy while staying within your budget?

Group 1: Chicken, potatoes, avocados, strawberries
Group 2: Chicken, avocados, carrots, cherries
Group 3: Trout, carrots, avocados, strawberries

What to Cook?

A restaurant's menu tells customers what kind of food is available. Is it Mexican food? Asian food? Or simple soups and sandwiches? A chef wants to offer interesting food items that are different from what other restaurants serve. She wants customers to be excited about eating at her restaurant. She wants them to come back again and to tell their friends what a great restaurant they've found.

Setting Menu Prices

The chef has to figure out exactly how much she should charge customers for each item on the menu. How does she do this? First, she thinks about where her restaurant is located. Most of her customers will

These people at a restaurant study the menu to decide what to order.

be people who live in the neighborhood. She looks at other restaurants that are nearby. What types of food do they offer? How much do they charge?

Also, she figures out what it costs to make each item on her menu. This is very important. She needs to charge more for each item than what it costs, so that she will make a **profit**. Profit is the money that is left after she pays all of her expenses.

You Do the Math

How Much Should the Chef Charge?

Figure out what the chef should charge for each of these two dinners. To make a profit she needs to charge $10.00 more for each dinner than the cost of the ingredients. Look at the cost for each item and calculate the total cost for each dinner. Then calculate what the chef should charge.

Dinner #1	
Ingredient	**Cost**
Salmon	$6.00
Rice	$1.00
Carrots	$1.50
Sliced tomatoes	$1.50
Bread	$2.00

Dinner #2	
Ingredient	**Cost**
Pork chops	$3.00
Cheese potatoes	$1.50
Peas with onions	$1.00
Applesauce	$0.50
Biscuits	$1.00

Customers!

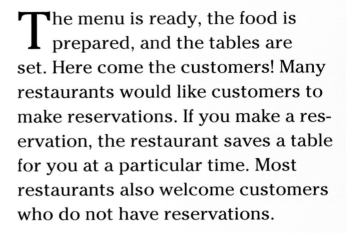

The menu is ready, the food is prepared, and the tables are set. Here come the customers! Many restaurants would like customers to make reservations. If you make a reservation, the restaurant saves a table for you at a particular time. Most restaurants also welcome customers who do not have reservations.

Keeping Track

Either way, the chef keeps track of how many people come to the restaurant. He also keeps track of what times of day and what days of the week the most people come in, so that he knows when he can expect the restaurant to be busiest. He uses all of the **data**, or information, to plan how much food to buy and to plan how many workers he needs at different times of day and on each of the days of the week.

When a restaurant is crowded, the servers are kept very busy bringing all of the customers their food.

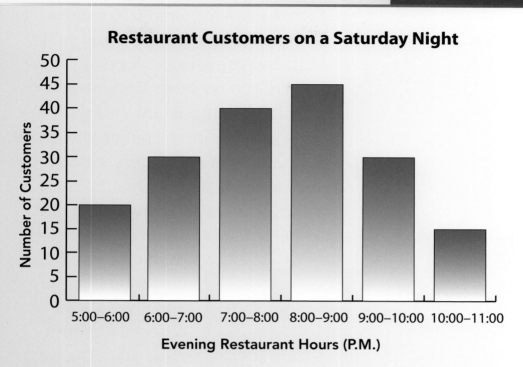

Restaurant Customers on a Saturday Night

(Bar graph: Number of Customers vs. Evening Restaurant Hours (P.M.))

- 5:00–6:00 — 20
- 6:00–7:00 — 30
- 7:00–8:00 — 40
- 8:00–9:00 — 45
- 9:00–10:00 — 30
- 10:00–11:00 — 15

A Busy Saturday Night

The chef has made a graph to show how many customers came into his restaurant during each hour on a recent Saturday night. Use the graph to answer the questions.

1. In which one-hour time period did the most customers come into the restaurant?

2. In which one-hour time period did the fewest customers come into the restaurant?

3. How many more customers came into the restaurant in the 8:00–9:00 P.M. hour than in the 5:00–6:00 P.M. hour?

4. How many fewer customers came into the restaurant in the 10:00–11:00 P.M. hour than in the 9:00–10:00 P.M. hour?

5. How many people in all came into the restaurant on this Saturday night?

The Restaurant Staff

Line cooks do some of the cooking, as well as washing and chopping the food, in a restaurant kitchen.

It takes a lot of people to make a restaurant successful. Line cooks wash and prepare the food and do some of the cooking. Many restaurants have an assistant chef who helps the executive chef as she cooks the main dishes. Greeters welcome customers and show them to their tables. Servers take the orders and deliver the food to the tables. A cashier takes the customers' money and gives them change. Busboys clear all of the dirty dishes off the tables and then reset the tables for new customers.

How Much They Earn

The executive chef generally earns the most money of all the workers in a restaurant. The assistant chef, who directly helps the executive chef, usually earns the next highest amount.

Most of the workers in a restaurant earn about the **minimum wage**. This is the least amount of money that a worker can be paid per hour. The minimum wage is set by law. In most cases, the greeter and the line cooks earn a little more than most other workers.

How Much Can Restaurant Workers Make?

How much could different types of restaurant workers earn for an 8-hour work shift? Use the table of wages below to answer the questions.

Workers and Wages	
Worker	**Hourly Wage**
Busboy	$ 8.00
Assistant chef	$20.00
Server	$ 9.00
Line cook	$12.00
Greeter	$10.00

1. Which type of worker listed in the table will earn the greatest amount of money in an 8-hour shift?

2. Which type of worker will earn the least amount of money?

3. For an 8-hour work shift, how much more will the greeter earn than the server?

4. For an 8-hour work shift, how much less does a line cook earn than the assistant chef?

5. How much will a server earn in one week if the server works 5 days, 8 hours each day?

Money In and Out

For a restaurant, income is the money that customers spend at the restaurant. Expenses are what the restaurant pays the workers and pays for the food and other needed items. Sometimes a restaurant has to buy new tablecloths, new pots, or new furniture. Usually, the restaurant owner also has to pay rent for the space where the restaurant is located.

Keeping Income Higher Than Expenses

A chef who owns or runs her own restaurant adds up her expenses and checks them

A cashier gives a customer his change after he pays for his food.

carefully to be sure she has enough income to pay for everything—and also has some money left over. This money left over is the restaurant's profit. Most chefs who own their own restaurants compare the restaurant's income to its expenses at least once a week.

Sometimes unexpected things happen. Perhaps fewer customers are coming into the restaurant for a few days because the weather is bad and everyone is staying home. Then, the restaurant's income goes down, and the chef has to adjust her expenses. She might ask some of the cooks to stay home or she might buy less food for a day or two, until the weather improves and business gets better.

You Do the Math

You Be the Cashier

You are the cashier at a restaurant. As customers pay for their dinner, you need to give them change. Look at the table of customers and what each customer's check is (the check is a piece of paper that shows how much customers have to pay). If each customer hands you a $100 bill, how much change will you give each person?

Customers and Check Amounts	
Customer	**Check Amount**
Customer A	$65.00
Customer B	$38.00
Customer C	$82.00
Customer D	$71.00
Customer E	$44.00

Starting a Restaurant

Many chefs would like to own their own restaurant. To be successful, a chef will first need a good plan for how to make the restaurant popular. It should be in a place where many people will see it. It should have food that customers will find interesting and will enjoy. The chef needs to plan for all of these things.

Then, he must be organized as he purchases equipment, creates the menu, and hires people to work for him. He must also have excellent math skills. Last, he should be willing to work very, very hard!

A Long To-Do List

Some chefs will decide to buy a restaurant from someone else. This can make it easier to get the restaurant open quickly, because the kitchen equipment and such things as the tables, chairs, dishes, and glasses will be included

Famous chef Wolfgang Puck shows children how to toss pizza dough at the grand opening of one of his restaurants.

in the purchase price of the restaurant. If a chef opens a brand new restaurant, he'll need to buy all of the things needed to run the business.

Either way, the chef needs to plan his menu and what he'll charge for each item. Then, he needs to advertise, or let people know his restaurant is opening. He might put an ad in the local newspaper or hand out notices in the neighborhood. Advertising adds to the cost of starting a restaurant.

You Do the Math

How Much People Spend at Restaurants

Many people enjoy going to restaurants. Look at the bar graph that shows how much money people spent in restaurants across the United States in the years 1970, 1980, 1990, and 2000. Then use the graph to answer the questions.

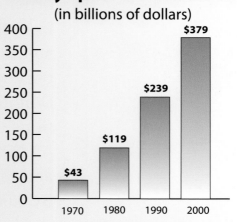

Money Spent in Restaurants
(in billions of dollars)

Source: National Restaurant Association

1. How much more money was spent in restaurants in 2000 than in 1990?

2. What was the increase in the amount of money spent between 1970 and 1980?

3. What is the **difference** in the amounts of money spent in the year with the greatest amount of sales and in the year with the least amount of sales?

4. How many years does the graph cover?

A Day in the Life of a Chef

What is it like to be a chef? Let's spend the day with Chef Donna and see! She's at the fresh food market by 6:00 A.M. She looks at the boxes of fruits and vegetables, as she thinks about what she'll cook that day. She picks the items that look the freshest.

A chef tastes one of the day's menu items to make sure it has been prepared just right.

Planning the Day

When Donna gets to the restaurant, she plans the evening's menu choices, which she changes nightly. She orders shrimp, salmon, and lobster from the fish purveyor. She orders steaks and chicken from the meat purveyor. The assistant chef arrives. Donna reviews the evening's reservations. It's going to be busy tonight. All the line cooks arrive by 3:00 P.M., and they're given their assignments. By 5:00 P.M., the chefs have prepared sample plates of the evening's menu items. Donna tastes them to see if anything needs to be changed to make each dish perfect. Then, the doors open and the evening of serving customers begins.

The Chef's Schedule

Look at Chef Donna's **schedule**. See if you can answer the questions.

Chef Donna's Schedule	
Time	**Activity**
6:00–7:30 A.M.	Shop at the fresh food market.
8:00–9:00 A.M.	Arrive at the restaurant. Unload food. Check amounts of food on hand.
9:00–10:15 A.M.	Plan the menu.
10:15–10:45 A.M.	Place orders with fish and meat purveyors.
10:45–11:45 A.M.	Meet with the assistant chef. Discuss menu.
12:00 P.M.	Begin cooking.
3:00–4:00 P.M.	Meet with arriving line cooks. Assign jobs.
5:00 P.M.	Taste sample plates.
5:30 P.M.	Doors open! The first customers arrive.
5:30–10:00 P.M.	Cook. Oversee kitchen and other chefs.
10:00 P.M.	The restaurant closes.
11:00 P.M.	After everyone cleans up, Chef Donna goes home.

1. How much time does Chef Donna spend meeting with line cooks and the assistant chef before the restaurant opens?

2. How many hours long is Chef Donna's working day?

3. How much time does she spend planning the menu?

4. How much time does she spend obtaining food from the fresh food market and from purveyors?

Personal Chefs

If you like cooking and working with people but you don't want to work the long hours that many restaurant chefs do, you might want to be a personal chef. A personal chef often works for individuals or families. These people are the chef's **clients**.

The chef meets with each client to decide on a week's menu. The client and the chef will agree on how much the chef will spend on food. After that, the chef will shop for the food and then cook it in the family's home. The chef leaves dinner in

A personal chef prepares a meal in a client's kitchen.

the refrigerator, along with instructions for the client about how to reheat it.

Special Meal Planning

Many people want meals that meet special diet needs. The chef might need to cook dishes that are low in calories. Some clients may need meals that are especially low in fat or low in salt. It is important for the chef to know a lot about **nutrition**, so that she can suggest ideas for dinner that meet the needs of her client.

You Do the Math

How Does a Personal Chef Make Money?

Most personal chefs charge a set fee to shop for and cook the meals. The cost of the food they buy is extra. Chef Joan has 4 clients she cooks for every week.

Client 1: Prepare 5 dinners for 4 people. Fee: $300.00

Client 2: Prepare 5 dinners for 2 people. Fee: $150.00

Client 3: Prepare 4 dinners for 2 people. Fee: $120.00

Client 4: Prepare 5 dinners for 1 person. Fee: $75.00

1. How much money will Chef Joan earn in 1 week?

2. How much money will she earn in 4 weeks?

3. How much money would she make in 1 week if she could add another client who needed 5 dinners for 4 people for a fee of $300.00?

4. Client 4 goes on vacation for 1 week and doesn't need Chef Joan to cook for him. How much money will the chef earn from her first 3 clients that week?

Caterers

Make the client happy! That's the job of the caterer. A chef who is a caterer works with clients who are having a party for a wedding, graduation, birthday, or other special occasion. The client tells the caterer the number of guests who will be attending. The client and caterer then decide on a budget—that is, how much money the client will pay the caterer. The client and caterer will also decide what food the caterer will serve and what the caterer's responsibilities will be. Sometimes the caterer provides just the food. For other parties, the caterer also takes care of providing the

Caterers very carefully carry the wedding cake into the party.

decorations, the tables, chairs, and dishes, and the people to serve and clean up.

Being Organized

A caterer can be creative and have fun with his work. He has to be good at planning and organizing. He manages his schedule carefully so that the food is ready and delivered to the party on time. He also has to be ready for last-minute changes. The number of guests may change. Or an outdoor party may have to be moved indoors because of rain. On the day of the party, the caterer and his staff are very busy.

You Do the Math

Catering a Wedding

A caterer has been hired for a wedding with 100 guests. The client needs to choose which dinner menu she wants to serve. The caterer charges a set fee for each guest's dinner that the client orders.

Menu 1: Roast chicken, rice, green beans, fresh fruit
  Fee: $20.00 per guest

Menu 2: Steak, baked potato, salad, French bread
  Fee: $40.00 per guest

Menu 3: Fresh fish, carrots, salad, dinner roll
  Fee: $25.00 per guest

1. If the client selects Menu 2, how much will the caterer charge?

2. If the client selects Menu 3, how much will the caterer charge?

3. How much less will Menu 1 cost the client than Menu 2?

4. If the client orders 50 Menu 1 dinners, and 50 Menu 2 dinners, what will the caterer charge?

If You Want to Be a Chef

To be a successful chef, you need to enjoy cooking and creating new recipes with many different foods. It can be hard work, and the hours can be long. You will likely work evenings and weekends. You need to be organized. You need to be able to manage your own time and the time of workers you hire. It helps if you can keep calm while dealing with unexpected situations that come up.

While you are in high school, take lots of math classes. Chefs need to use math all the time as they make menu selections and work with recipes, as they look at data about customers, and as they keep track of their expenses and income.

After high school, you could attend a **culinary school**. Here, you will be trained in everything you need to know to be a chef. You'll be able to work in the culinary school's restaurant, where students learn how to be chefs by doing the job with real customers.

Answer Key

Pages 4-5: The Business of Cooking:
Calculate start time by counting back from the end time: cheese potatoes: 5:15; glazed carrots: 6:00; bread pudding: 5:30; roast chicken: 4:30; buttermilk biscuits: 6:10; pumpkin bread: 5:40. Sequential order: roast chicken, cheese potatoes, bread pudding, pumpkin bread, glazed carrots, buttermilk biscuits.

Pages 6-7: Kitchen Math:
Multiply each amount by 2 to double the recipe for oatmeal raisin cookies: 2 eggs, 2 cups sugar, 3 cups oats, 1 cup butter, 4 tablespoons milk, $\frac{1}{2}$ cup raisins. Divide each amount by 2 to halve the recipe for French toast: 2 slices bread, 1 egg, $\frac{1}{4}$ cup milk, 1 tablespoon butter.

Pages 8-9: Cooking Supplies:
For items 1, 2, and 3: current temperature of food – correct temperature = amount temperature has to be lowered. Roast beef: 48 – 41 = 7. Shrimp: 60 – 34 = 26. Lettuce: 51 – 41 = 10. For items 4 and 5: safe temperature – current temperature = amount temperature can go up. Flour: 70 – 45 = 25. Sugar: 70 – 60 = 10.

Pages 10-11: Buying the Food:
Add the costs of the items in each group. **Group 1:** $17.00 + $12.00 + $17.00 + $24.00 = $70.00. **Group 2:** $17.00 + $17.00 + $20.00 + $35.00 = $89.00. **Group 3:** $24.00 + $20.00 + $17.00 + $24.00 = $85.00. Group 1 costs $70.00. This is the chef's budget. She can buy Group 1. Groups 2 and 3 cost too much.

Pages 12-13: What to Cook?
The total cost of the ingredients + $10.00 = the menu price. **Dinner #1:** $22.00. (The cost is $6.00 + $1.00 + $1.50 + $1.50 + $2.00 = $12.00. The menu price is $12.00 + $10.00 = $22.00.) **Dinner #2:** $17.00. (The cost is $3.00 + $1.50 + $1.00 + $0.50 + $1.00 = $7.00. The menu price is $7.00 + $10.00 = $17.00.)

Pages 14-15: Customers!
Compare the totals for each bar. **1.** More customers came in during the 8:00–9:00 P.M. hour than during any other. **2.** Fewer customers came in during the 10:00–11:00 P.M. hour than during any other. **3.** 25 (45 – 20 = 25). **4.** 15 (30 – 15 = 15). **5.** 180 (20 + 30 + 40 + 45 + 30 + 15 = 180).

Pages 16-17: The Restaurant Staff:
Multiply 8 hours x a worker's hourly wage to find the daily earnings for that type of worker. **1.** Assistant chef. **2.** Busboy. **3.** The greeter earns $8.00 more. (The greeter earns $10.00 x 8 = $80.00. The server earns $9.00 x 8 = $72.00. Then, $80.00 – $72.00 = $8.00.) **4.** The line cook earns $64.00 less. (The line cook earns $12.00 x 8 = $96.00. The assistant chef earns $20.00 x 8 = $160.00. Then, $160.00 – $96.00 = $64.00.) **5.** $360.00 (for 5 days the server earns $72.00 x 5 = $360.00).

Pages 18-19: Money In and Out:
$100.00 – the check = the amount of change. **A:** $35.00. **B:** $62.00. **C:** $18.00. **D:** $29.00. **E:** $56.00.

Pages 20-21: Starting a Restaurant:
Subtract the smaller amount from the larger amount to get the difference. **1.** $140 billion ($379 – $239 = $140). **2.** $76 billion ($119 – $43 = $76). **3.** $336 billion (the greatest sales were in 2000: $379 billion; the least sales were in 1970: $43 billion; $379 – $43 = $336). **4.** 30 years (2000 – 1970 = 30).

Pages 22-23: A Day in the Life of a Chef:
1. 2 hours (10:45–11:45 A.M. is 1 hour, and 3:00–4:00 P.M. is 1 hour). **2.** 6:00 A.M. to 11 P.M. = 17 hours. **3.** 9:00–10:15 A.M. = 1 hour 15 minutes. **4.** 2 hours (6:00–7:30 A.M. is $1\frac{1}{2}$ hours, and 10:15–10:45 is $\frac{1}{2}$ hour).

Pages 24-25: Personal Chefs:
1. $300 + $150 + $120 + $75 = $645. **2.** $645 x 4 = $2,580. **3.** $645 + $300 = $945. **4.** $645 – $75 = $570.

Pages 26-27: Caterers:
1. 100 guests x $40 = $4,000. **2.** 100 guests x $25 = $2,500. **3.** $2,000 less (Menu 2: 100 guests x $40 = $4000; Menu 1: 100 guests x $20 = $2,000; then, $4,000 – $2,000 = $2,000). **4.** $3,000 (50 guests x $20 = $1,000, and 50 guests x $40 = $2,000.00; then, $1,000 + $2,000 = $3,000).

Glossary

calculate—To figure out the exact answer to a problem.

client—A person, group of people, or company for whom a chef or other professional performs services.

convert—To change something, such as the amounts in a recipe.

culinary school—A school where people learn about cooking and working as a chef.

data—Information collected about people or things.

difference—The amount by which one number is greater than another number.

estimating—Figuring out about how many or how much.

ingredients—The foods that go into a recipe.

minimum wage—The lowest amount of money that a worker can be paid per hour in the United States; it is set by law.

nutrition—The study of food and the things foods contain (for example, calories, fat, vitamins, and minerals).

profit—The income that a business has left after it pays all of its expenses.

purveyor—A person or company that supplies food or other goods.

recipe—Directions for preparing something to eat.

refrigerated—Kept cold, usually by being stored in a refrigerator.

schedule—A list of activities or events and the time at which each one happens.

sequential order—The order in which things happen.

thermometer—An instrument for measuring temperature.

To Learn More

Read these books:

Discovering Careers for Your Future—Food. New York: J.G. Ferguson Publishing, 2005.

Klein, Hilary. *A Day with a Chef.* Mankato, Minn.: Child's World, 2008.

Maze, Stephanie. *I Want to Be a Chef.* San Diego, Calif.: Harcourt Brace, 1999.

Look up these Web sites:

Chefs A'Field
http://www.chefsafield.com

CIA (Culinary Institute of America)
http://www.ciakids.com

Junior Chefs of America
http://www.jrchefsofamerica.com

Key Internet search terms:

chef, cooking, food, restaurant

Index

About the Author

Sheri L. Arroyo has a master of arts degree in education. She has been an elementary school teacher in San Diego, California, for more than twenty years and has taught third grade for the past thirteen years.

The Declaration of Independence

How 13 Colonies Became the United States

The Declaration of Independence

How 13 Colonies Became the United States

Written by **Syl Sobel**

Illustrated by Denise Gilgannon

BARRON'S

Barron's Educational Series, Inc.

To Joan

You're the best!

Acknowledgments

I wish to thank my colleague, Dr. Bruce Ragsdale, for reviewing my manuscripts and offering valuable suggestions. My wife, Joan, and daughters, Mo and Izzy, read various drafts with critical eyes and offered sound advice. Any errors that may appear in the text are entirely mine.

All inquiries should be addressed to:
Barron's Educational Series, Inc.
250 Wireless Boulevard
Hauppauge, New York 11788
www.barronseduc.com

ISBN-13: 978-0-7641-3950-5
ISBN-10: 0-7641-3950-9

Library of Congress Catalog Card No. 2007043769

Library of Congress Cataloging-in-Publication Data
    Sobel, Syl.
      The Declaration of Independence : how 13 colonies became the United States / by Syl Sobel.
        p.   cm.
    Includes bibliographical references.
      1. United States. Declaration of Independence—Juvenille literature.
    2. United States—Politics and government—1775–1783—Juvenile literature.
    I. Title.
    E221.S64   2008
    973.3'13—dc20   2007043769

Printed in China
9 8 7 6 5 4 3 2 1

Contents

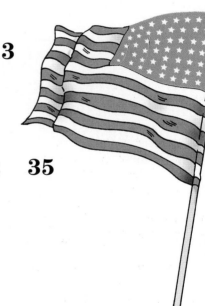

Introduction

Every year Americans celebrate on July 4th with fireworks, fairs, picnics, parades, and other festive events. Some people call it America's Birthday. Other people call it Independence Day. Why are we celebrating the Fourth of July? We are celebrating something that happened back in 1776.

The United States in 1776 was not like the big country we know today. Instead of fifty states, there were only thirteen. They were not called *states* back then either. They were called *colonies*, which means they belonged to another country—England. Even though each colony had its own government, the colonies were still part of England and colonists still had to obey British laws.

By 1776, however, many colonists did not want to belong to England any more. They did not want to follow British laws. They wanted the colonies to become free and independent.

Taxation Without Representation

Trouble started in the 1760s. England had fought a war with France from 1756 to 1763 to win control of Canada and other parts of North America. That war was called the Seven Years' War or the French and Indian War. England won, but the war was costly, and the British government needed money.

King George III

King George III of England and his advisers decided to make colonists pay taxes to the British government. After all, one reason for the war was to protect the American colonies. British leaders thought the colonies should pay for that protection.

First, the British government made a law that the colonists had to pay taxes for sugar. Then they made a law that the colonists had to buy tax stamps to put on all printed material. This meant the colonists had to buy stamps for newspapers, marriage licenses, even calendars and playing cards.

"Unfair," the colonists protested. It was not just the money that made them mad. The colonists did not think it was fair for a country 3,000 miles across the ocean to tell them what to do. "That's taxation without representation," colonists complained. That means the British government made laws requiring colonists to pay taxes even though the colonists did not have *representatives* in England helping to make the laws.

At first, King George and the British leaders listened to the colonists' complaints. They removed most of the taxes. But they still wanted to show the colonists that they were in charge.

"This is the Mother Country," said one British leader. "They are the children. They must obey."

So England kept one important tax—a tax on tea.

Boston Tea Party

Colonists were angry. They loved tea. It was their favorite beverage. But it was not just the tax that made the colonists mad. The tax on tea was really quite small—only three cents a pound. Colonists were mad because they did not like the British government bossing them around. Many colonists refused to buy the British tea, making homemade beverages instead.

Then, on a winter night in December 1773, a group of boys and men, many of them disguised as Mohawk Indians, boarded British ships loaded with tea in Boston Harbor and dumped the tea overboard.

King George and British leaders were furious. This *Boston Tea Party*, as it was called, was a challenge to their authority.

"Criminals," one British nobleman said of the Bostonians.

The king agreed. The colonists had to be punished. "We must master them," he said.

The British government made strict new laws for Massachusetts. Colonists in Massachusetts could no longer elect their own leaders or make their own laws. The king put the British military in charge of Massachusetts. Worse, the colonists had to provide housing for British soldiers, even if that meant letting the soldiers stay in their homes.

The British also closed Boston Harbor until the colonists paid for the tea that was dumped into the harbor. Residents of Boston and throughout Massachusetts depended on fishing and shipping. Closing the port would ruin their businesses and would keep food and other supplies from coming into Boston.

News of these harsh laws spread throughout the colonies. King George had expected that these laws would frighten the other colonies into obeying the British government. Instead, however, the harsh treatment of Massachusetts helped to unite the colonies against England.

"If the British can punish Massachusetts, they can punish the rest of us," the colonists thought. Leaders of the colonies decided that they needed to work together.

First Continental Congress

Colonial leaders agreed to meet in Philadelphia in 1774. Every colony except Georgia sent representatives. They called this meeting the *First Continental Congress*. The colonies had never really tried to work together before. People from some colonies did not like people from some other colonies. Colonists also disagreed about their relationship with England.

Many colonists, called *patriots*, wanted independence from England. They did not want to obey British laws and pay taxes to the king. Patriots thought it was time for the colonies to work together like a team to break free from England. The differences "between Virginians, Pennsylvanians, New Yorkers, and New Englanders are no more," Patrick Henry of Virginia said. "I am not a Virginian, but an American."

Other colonists, however, wanted to get along with England. These colonists, called *loyalists*, still considered themselves loyal British subjects. After all, most of the colonists were either born in England, Scotland, or Ireland or had ancestors from there. The colonies had the same language, culture, and government as the British. Some colonists went to school in England, and many still had friends and family there.

Many colonists also had close business connections with England (largely because of British laws that required the colonies to trade with England). The colonies sent products such as sugar, tobacco, cotton, and wool to England. England sent manufactured products such as furniture, glass, paper, and clothes to the colonies. Many colonists depended on this trade.

Loyalists also liked the protection of the British Empire. England was the most powerful country in the world. Many colonists wanted the British army and navy to protect them from Native Americans and from French and Spanish settlers in other parts of North America.

Because of all these differences, this first Congress could not agree on much. They argued a lot. John Adams of Massachusetts, a lawyer and leading patriot, wrote in his diary that there was much "nibbling and quibbling" among the members of Congress.

Eventually, Congress sent a message to King George demanding an end to the unpopular laws. The king refused. The colonists must show "obedience to the Mother Country," he said, even if that meant war.

John Adams

Shot Heard 'Round the World

And so, the colonists prepared for war. In Massachusetts, patriots began gathering weapons and ammunition and training to fight. "Give me liberty or give me death," said Patrick Henry at a meeting of Virginia leaders.

Patriots knew they were putting their lives at risk by fighting the British. King George had offered rewards for the death or capture of patriot leaders. Taking on the powerful British army and navy would be very dangerous and difficult.

In April 1775, British troops in Boston learned that patriots were hiding weapons and ammunition in nearby Concord, Massachusetts. They sent soldiers to seize the supplies and to capture patriot leaders, who in the eyes of the British were outlaws and rebels.

Patriots poured from their homes and farms to fight the British. Early on April 19, 1775, a small group of patriots met British troops at the village green in Lexington, Massachusetts. Though no one is sure who fired first, the first military battle between the British and Americans took place. The British troops forced the patriots to flee from Lexington; they then continued their march to Concord. By the time the British got there later that day, however, the patriots had hidden most of their weapons and supplies. Patriots fought the British again at Concord and all the way back to Boston. Many British soldiers were killed or wounded. What became known as "the shot heard 'round the world" had been fired. The War for Independence had begun.

Decision in Philadelphia

In May 1775, a few weeks after the battles at Lexington and Concord, leaders of the colonies gathered again in the Pennsylvania State House in Philadelphia for the *Second Continental Congress*. This time, all thirteen colonies sent representatives.

The most respected leaders of the colonies were there. John Adams was there. So were his fiery cousin, Samuel Adams (one of the leaders of the Boston Tea Party), wealthy businessman John Hancock, also of Massachusetts, and wise and witty writer, newspaper publisher, and inventor Benjamin Franklin of Pennsylvania. So was the quiet and thoughtful young lawyer, Thomas Jefferson of Virginia.

Benjamin Franklin

One man who was not there was tall and commanding George Washington of Virginia. Washington had earned a reputation as a military leader when he fought for the British in the Seven Years' War. One of the first things the Second Continental Congress did soon after they began meeting was to choose Washington to lead a *Continental Army*. Up until then, each colony had its own army. But now, Congress decided to form an army with troops from all of the colonies. While the others met in Philadelphia, Washington and his army were preparing to fight the British.

Even with war underway, not all of the members of the Second Continental Congress were quite ready to declare independence from England. There were still many loyalists in the colonies. Some members of Congress still hoped to find a peaceful solution.

Thomas Jefferson

But the gap between England and the colonies was getting wider. Washington's army had forced the British army and many loyalists to leave Boston. This made the British even more determined to teach the colonists a lesson. Their army and navy gathered in Canada, preparing to invade the colonies. England hired thousands of German soldiers called Hessians to help them fight the rebels.

By the middle of 1776, patriots had taken control of every colony. Most colonists were for independence and ready for war.

On June 7, 1776, Richard Henry Lee of Virginia stood up to speak in Congress. Lee had instructions from the Virginia legislature to ask Congress to vote for independence. "These United Colonies are, and of right, ought to be, free and independent States," Lee said. He asked Congress to vote to free the colonies "from all allegiance to the British crown."

John Adams was delighted. He seconded what became known as the *Lee Resolution* (a resolution is an idea or statement that someone asks an official body such as Congress to support). The members of Congress asked Adams, Thomas Jefferson, Ben Franklin, Roger Sherman of Connecticut, and Robert Livingston of New York to write a *declaration* explaining why the colonies wanted their independence from England.

Adams and Jefferson had great respect for each other. Adams thought Jefferson had a sharp mind and was an excellent writer. Jefferson admired the older Adams as a wise mentor. Jefferson suggested that Adams write the Declaration, but Adams refused and told Jefferson that he should write it.

"What can be your reasons?" asked Jefferson.

Adams replied: "Reason first—You are a Virginian, and a Virginian ought to appear at the head of this business. Reason second—I am obnoxious . . . and unpopular. You are very much otherwise. Reason third—You can write ten times better than I can."

Jefferson took the job. What he wrote (with changes from Franklin and Adams, and more changes by Congress) is called the Declaration of Independence. It explains why colonists believed they had the right to declare independence from England. Here is what it said.

". . . united States"

From its opening title, the Declaration of Independence made clear that the colonies' connections with England were broken and could not be fixed. The Declaration was called "The unanimous Declaration of the thirteen united States of America." The word "States" was very important. Until then, Massachusetts, Pennsylvania, Virginia, and the others were considered "colonies" of England, which means they were under British rule. Calling them "States" meant that they were free and independent from England.

Calling the states "united" was also important. Colonists usually thought of themselves as citizens of their own colony. Each colony had its own government, its own laws, its own army, even its own type of money. The colonies were usually not "united" about much of anything. But calling themselves "united" in the Declaration showed that they were "one people" working together for one purpose—freedom from England.

In CONGRESS, July 4, 1776.

The unanimous Declaration of the thirteen united States of America

"... consent of the governed"

Next, the Declaration explained why the states wanted their freedom. It said that a government gets its power from the *consent of the governed*. Today we almost take for granted that the people of the United States—the "governed"—give the government its power. In 1776, however, the idea that a government got its power from the people was very new. Most countries were ruled by kings, queens, or other monarchs who either inherited their power or took it by force. Ordinary people usually believed they had to do whatever the government wanted them to do.

Colonial leaders, however, believed firmly in the new, revolutionary idea called *self-government*. They believed, as the Declaration of Independence said, that the people give the government its power, and the people can take it away.

The Declaration said that all people have certain rights, including "Life, Liberty, and the pursuit of Happiness." It said the people create a government to protect these rights. If the government uses its power improperly and takes these rights away, the Declaration said the people have the right to start a new government.

Of course, the Declaration said, people should not change governments without a good reason. Then it described many *abuses* or bad actions by King George, which it said gave the people of the United States the right to start their own government.

"... imposing Taxes ... without our Consent"

One of the king's abuses was "imposing Taxes on us without our Consent." As said earlier, however, the taxes were mostly quite small. It was not just the taxes that angered the colonists; it was that the tax laws were made "without our Consent." Congress was declaring that the colonists had a right to govern themselves, including having representatives to make tax laws and other laws. "Taxation without representation" was unacceptable.

"...absolute Tyranny over these States"

The Declaration then described other ways in which King George refused to allow the colonists to govern themselves. For example, even though each colony had its own congress or legislature, the king had the right to approve or reject laws that the colonial legislatures made. Sometimes, the Declaration said, the king "refused his Assent to Laws . . . for the public good." (Assent means "approval.") Sometimes the king "refused to pass other Laws . . . unless [the] people would [give up] the right of Representation in the Legislature."

Most of the colonies had a governor appointed by the king. But the colonial governors had to follow the king's orders. Sometimes, the Declaration said, "the king would not let his Governors pass Laws" that were important to the colonists.

Several times, when a colonial legislature was discussing a subject that the king did not want them to discuss, he ordered them to stop or prevented them from meeting. So the Declaration described how the king "dissolved Representative

Houses repeatedly" and "suspend[ed] our own Legislatures, and declar[ed the British government] invested with power to legislate for us."

The Declaration accused King George of "tyranny," which means that he was acting as an all-powerful ruler and violating the people's right to govern themselves.

"...obstructed the Administration of Justice"

Colonists were also angry that King George controlled the colonial courts. British authorities could arrest colonists and put them in jail for no reason. Sometimes, they would keep people in jail for a long time without telling them what crime they committed. So the Declaration of Independence described several ways in which the king abused his power by interfering with the colonists' right to have fair trials.

For example, the Declaration accused the king of "depriving us . . . of the benefit of Trial by Jury." (A *jury* is a group of regular people who decide whether someone accused of a crime is guilty.) It said the king "made Judges dependent on his Will alone" for how long they would have their jobs and for how much they would get paid. Colonists believed that judges who were hired and could be fired by the king would be more likely to decide cases in favor of the king and against the colonists.

". . . waging War against us"

Finally, the Declaration's list of abuses described how the king was using British military power against the colonists. It said the king put "Armies" of British soldiers in the colonies, without the consent of the colonial legislatures. The British forced colonists to let the soldiers live in their homes. The Declaration said the king put the militaryleaders in charge of the colonial governments and protected British soldiers from crimes they committed against the colonists.

"He has plundered our seas, ravaged our coasts, burnt our towns, and destroyed the lives of our people," the Declaration said. It said the king had hired soldiers from other countries

to bring more "death, desolation, and tyranny." It also accused the king of encouraging "the inhabitants of our frontiers"—Native Americans—to attack the colonists. The Declaration said that because King George was "waging War against" the colonies, he lost his right to govern them.

". . . our Lives, our Fortunes and our sacred Honor"

The Declaration described how the colonists had asked King George to stop his abuses, but the king only answered with "repeated injury." It said the king's actions made him a

"Tyrant . . . unfit to be the ruler of a free people." So, the Declaration concluded:

- "these United Colonies are, and of Right ought to be Free and Independent States,"
- the colonies no longer owe "Allegiance to the British Crown,"
- "all political connection between [the colonies] and the State of Great Britain, is and ought to be totally dissolved,"
- "and . . . as Free and Independent States," the colonies "have full Power to levy War . . . and to do all other

Acts and Things which Independent States may of right do."

The members of the Continental Congress knew that what they were doing was dangerous. No colonies had ever broken free of a great kingdom before. Colonists who fought against England would be committing the crime of *treason,* which means being disloyal to their country. The king had offered rewards to kill or capture the leaders of the revolution.

Nevertheless, on July 2, 1776, the Second Continental Congress voted for Richard Henry Lee's resolution for independence. On July 4, after making many changes to Jefferson's original version of the Declaration of Independence, representatives from twelve of the colonies voted to approve it. (New York approved it a few days later.)

Congress had a formal, handwritten version of the Declaration prepared on fancy parchment. In August 1776, fifty-six members of the Second Continental Congress signed it. John Hancock, the president of the Congress, was the first to sign. He wrote his name in big, fancy letters so that (according to legend) King George could read it without his eyeglasses.

One by one, members of Congress signed the document, sealing with their signatures this solemn vow in the Declaration's final words: "[W]e mutually pledge to each other our Lives, our Fortunes and our sacred Honor." As Ben Franklin said: "We must all hang together, or assuredly we shall all hang separately."

Independence!

Congress had copies of the Declaration made, and it was read throughout the states. On July 9, George Washington had a copy read to his troops, who were now in New York preparing to fight the British invasion. Soldiers and other patriots were so inspired that they tore down a large statue of King George. Lead from the statue was later used to make bullets for the patriots.

To the British, the Declaration of Independence was a declaration of treason. To them, it meant the leaders of the colonies were openly rebelling against the king and had to be punished.

The war continued for five more years. The British drove Washington and his army out of New York, chased them through New Jersey, into Pennsylvania, and eventually captured Philadelphia. The Continental Army suffered a long, hard winter of 1777 in Valley Forge, outside of Philadelphia. But Washington and his troops kept hanging on, fighting small battles, and wearing down the British. Finally, with the help of French soldiers and warships, the United States won its independence from England in 1783.

Creating the U.S. Government

The Declaration of Independence declared that the states were united in working together for their freedom. But it did not create a government for the United States. The thirteen states first tried working together under an agreement called the Articles of Confederation. But that did not work very well. Each state had its own laws, but there were no laws for all of the states, no government for all of the states, and no way to raise money to pay for an army.

By 1787, the leaders of the states decided they needed to work together as one nation. These early leaders—who along

with the signers of the Declaration are called the *Founders* or the *Framers*—decided to write rules for a new national government. They called those rules the Constitution of the United States.

The Founders who wrote the Constitution remembered King George's abuses. They did not want a government like King George's. They did not want their new government to become too powerful. They wanted to protect the people's rights. So the Founders put many ideas from the Declaration of Independence into the Constitution to tell the government what it can do and, just as important, what it cannot do.

The Founders believed, for example, that the government must get its power from what the Declaration called "the

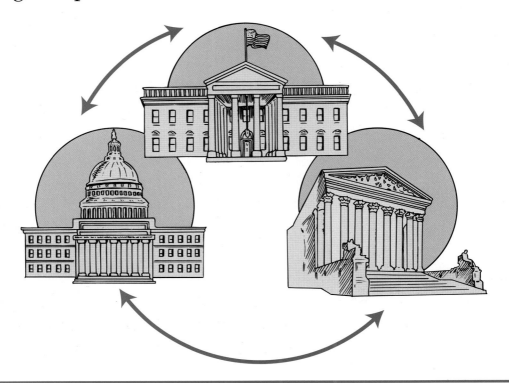

consent of the governed." So the Constitution began with "We the People of the United States . . . do . . . establish this Constitution," to show that the people create the U.S. government and give the government its power.

The Founders remembered how King George used his power to become what the Declaration called a "tyrant." They did not want one person or one part of their new government to become too powerful. So the Constitution created a government that divides power among three parts, which are called branches.

The Founders remembered how important the "right of representation" was in the Declaration of Independence. They knew that it was unfair for the British government to make laws for the colonies without allowing the colonists to have representatives helping to make the laws. So the first branch of government created by the Constitution is the lawmaking or legislative branch, called Congress. People from each state elect individuals to represent them in Congress and to make laws, including laws about taxes.

The Founders knew a government needed a leader, but they did not want any one person in the government to become too powerful, like a king. So they created a second branch called the executive branch, which is led by the president. The Constitution gave the president and the executive branch the job of carrying out the laws that Congress makes. But to keep the president from becoming too powerful, the Constitution said an election for president must be held every four years.

The Founders remembered that fair courts and fair trials were also important rights mentioned in the Declaration. So the Constitution created a third branch of government, called the judicial branch, which contains the courts. The Constitution has many rules that protect the rights of people who are accused of committing crimes.

Conclusion

The states approved the Constitution in 1787, and the national government of the United States of America was created. General George Washington was elected the first president of the United States. John Adams was the second president. Thomas Jefferson was the third.

The Philadelphia State House, where the Second Continental Congress met and declared independence, became known as Independence Hall. That formal version of the Declaration signed by Hancock and fifty-five other members of Congress is now on display at the National Archives in Washington, D.C. A signature is often called a "John Hancock."

We celebrate what the Declaration means every year on July 4, which is known as Independence Day. (John Adams wrote in a letter to his wife that he thought July 2, the day the Second Continental Congress voted for independence, would be the day that Americans would always celebrate.)

The Declaration of Independence is more than just some important-sounding words on a fancy piece of parchment. It tells the world what the Founders of our country believed about government—that people have rights, that a government gets its power from the people, and that the government's job is to protect the people's rights. These ideas are still at the heart of how our government works today. That is why we celebrate on the Fourth of July.

Glossary

Abuses
Bad actions by a leader, such as the actions by King George III that caused the colonists to declare independence from England.

Boston Tea Party
In December 1773, to protest the British tax on tea, a group of boys and men boarded British ships loaded with tea in Boston Harbor and dumped the tea overboard.

Colony
A settlement or territory that belongs to another country.

Consent of the governed
The idea that the people create their government and give the government its power.

Continental Army
The army made up of soldiers from all of the colonies, which the Second Continental Congress created and appointed George Washington to lead.

Declaration
An official statement by a governing body. The Second Continental Congress approved the Declaration of Independence.

First Continental Congress
A group of representatives from twelve colonies who met in Philadelphia in 1774. They sent a letter to King George III asking him to end certain taxes and other unpopular laws the British government had placed on the colonies.

Founders or Framers
The signers of the Declaration of Independence and the Constitution and other early leaders of the United States.

Jury
A group of regular people who decide whether someone accused of a crime is guilty.

Lee Resolution
The request by Richard Henry Lee of Virginia for the Second Continental Congress to declare that the colonies were free and independent from England.

Loyalists
Colonists who still considered themselves loyal British subjects and opposed independence.

Patriots
American colonists who were for independence and prepared to fight, and eventually fought, against the British during the War for Independence.

Representatives
People who are selected to make laws or make other decisions on behalf of other people. For example, the people of the United States elect representatives to make laws for them in Congress.

Second Continental Congress
Representatives from thirteen colonies who met in Philadelphia starting in 1775 to decide whether the colonies wanted to declare independence from England. In July 1776, the Second Continental Congress voted in favor of independence and approved the Declaration of Independence.

Self-government
The idea that people decide for themselves what kind of government to form and what power to give it.

State
A place that has its own independent government.

Treason
The crime of being disloyal to your country. The British king and government thought the leaders of the American Revolution were committing treason against England.

Selected Bibliography

Many fine children's books are available about the Declaration of Independence and the Revolutionary War. Here are some of them.

Bober, Natalie S., *Countdown to Independence: A Revolution of Ideas in England and Her American Colonies: 1760–1776* (Atheneum Books, New York, 2001).

Bobrick, Benson, *Fight for Freedom: The American Revolutionary War* (Atheneum Books, New York, 2004).

Collier, Christopher and James Lincoln Collier, *The American Revolution* (Benchmark Books, Tarrytown, New York, 1998).

Dolan, Edward F., *The American Revolution: How We Fought the War of Independence* (Millbrook Press, Brookfield, CT, 1995).

Fink, Sam, *The Declaration of Independence* (Scholastic, New York, 2002).

Fritz, Jean, *Will You Sign Here, John Hancock?* (Scholastic, New York, 1987).

Hoff Oberlin, Loriann, *The Everything American History Book* (Adams Media, Avon, MA, 2001).

January, Brendan, *The Revolutionary War* (Childrens Press, New York, 2000).

Schanzer, Rosalyn, *George vs. George: The American Revolution As Seen from Both Sides* (National Geographic Society, Washington, DC, 2004).

St. George, Judith, *The Journey of the One and Only Declaration of Independence* (Philomel Books, New York, 2005).

Index

··

K

King George III
    abuses by, 24–25, 36, 41
    denial of self-governance by, 26
    description of, 8–10, 12, 15–16
    "tyranny" by, 28, 30–31, 37

L

Lee, Richard Henry, 20, 32
Lee Resolution, 20, 42
Legislature, 27
Lexington, 16–17
Livingston, Robert, 20
Loyalists, 14, 19, 43

M

Massachusetts, 10, 12, 16
Military abuses, 30

N

New Jersey, 34

P

Patriots, 14, 16, 43
Pennsylvania, 34
Philadelphia, 13
Philadelphia State House, 39
President, 37
Pursuit of Happiness, 24

R

"Repeated injury," 30
Representatives, 9, 43
"Right of representation," 37

S

Second Continental Congress, 18–19, 32, 39–40, 43
Self-governance, 26
Self-government, 23, 43
Seven Years' War, 8
Sherman, Roger, 20
Shot heard 'round the world, 16–17
"States," 21–22, 44

T

Taxes and taxation
    without consent, 25
    without representation, 8–9, 25
Tea, 9, 10–12
Treason, 32, 34, 44
Trial by Jury, 29–30
Tyranny, 28, 30–31, 37

U

"United" states, 22
U.S. government, 35–38

V

Valley Forge, 34

W

Washington, George, 18, 34, 39